100
THINGS TO DO IN
ATLANTA
BEFORE YOU
DIE

100

THINGS TO DO IN
ATLANTA
BEFORE YOU
DIE

• •

SARAH GLEIM

REEDY PRESS

Library of Congress Control Number: 2016937275

ISBN: 9781681060446

Design by Jill Halpin

Printed in the United States of America
16 17 18 19 20   5 4 3 2 1

Please note that websites, phone numbers, addresses, and company names are subject to change or cancellation. We did our best to relay the most accurate information available, but due to circumstances beyond our control, please do not hold us liable for misinformation. When exploring new destinations, please do your homework before you go.

CONTENTS

• •

Music and Entertainment

• •

Sports and Recreation

● ●

Culture and History

Shopping

PREFACE

So things have changed a lot in Atlanta since we released the first edition of this book just a few years ago. Tons of new restaurants and shops have opened, developments that were in the works are completed, and there's still so much progress and redevelopment, I could write another entire book on that alone! Some of the old-school Atlantans don't necessarily like all the changes; they think it brings in too many outsiders and adds to the traffic. But not me—I think the revitalization going on here is a fantastic thing for the city. I grew up here and have loved watching the changes to our skyline, and now more than ever I am thrilled to see the investment in neighborhoods that once stood vacant and rundown. The growth continues to encourage people from all over the country to come to Atlanta because it's a great place to work, live, and raise a family. And you simply can't beat the blend of people and cultures we have here.

So when I got the chance to update *100 Things to Do in Atlanta Before You Die*, I wanted to be sure it still captured everything I've come to know and appreciate about my home city, like Southern cuisine, Coca-Cola, and Civil Rights history. But also I wanted to add new and interesting spots that continue to make Atlanta the modern cultural center of the South. I'll admit, I remain amazed at how many quirky, historic, exciting, and even daring things exist here, and it's my job to always be in the know. You'll find obvious faves like the Georgia Aquarium, CNN, and Zoo Atlanta, but now that the research is completed for you and wrapped up in this handy book, all you have to do is start checking the other wild and crazy things off your list (how does driving a military tank sound?).

While I've added some killer new places, and sadly had to delete some that are gone, one thing absolutely remains the same about this list—it is not meant to rank the places in Atlanta from first to worst. Instead, it's 100 things (some a little more out there than others) that will give you good insight and appreciation for what makes Atlanta, well, Atlanta. So dig right in! It's full of itineraries for foodies, sports fans, art aficionados, and outdoor enthusiasts too. And if you're like me, there are still plenty of things in this book that I know you haven't checked off either. If you know of more ATL musts that are tops, let me know on Facebook at www. facebook.com/100ThingsATL. I definitely want to hear from you. As always, it's been a blast Atlanta! #ChooseAtl

—Sarah Gleim

FOOD AND DRINK

HAVE A CHILI DOG
AT THE VARSITY

What'll ya have? What'll ya have? Easy answer—a chili dog, F.O., and fried pie at the Varsity. The historic downtown drive-in is the world's largest, so skip the inside seating and park your car where you can delight in the show put on by the famous carhops. These "curb men" are as much a part of the experience here as washing down your onion rings with a Coca-Cola. Their job is to take your order, but they entertain while they do, singing the items on the menu, just as they have been doing since this landmark opened in 1928.

61 North Avenue, 404-881-1706, www.thevarsity.com
Neighborhood: Downtown

DRINK UP
AT THE WORLD OF COCA-COLA

You don't dare mention the "P" word in this town. Atlanta is, after all, the home of Coca-Cola. To get a taste of the real thing, tour the World of Coca-Cola, where you'll be surrounded by everything that has made this soft drink one of the world's most famous brands—from iconic Coca-Cola advertising to original artwork from Norman Rockwell and Howard Finster. No trip here would be complete without a few samples—and they're unlimited in the Tasting Room. You can sip nearly a hundred different Coca-Cola fountain drinks from around the world, so it's safe to say you'll definitely leave with a sugar rush.

121 Baker Street, 404-676-5151, www.worldofcoca-cola.com
Neighborhood: Downtown

BELLY UP
TO THE BAR

I love a good beer (see page 20 for two of my favorite spots), but sometimes you just gotta have a killer cocktail. And there's definitely no shortage of spots in town that serve up some stiff drinks and even better people watching. Holeman & Finch Public House has been setting the bar high since it opened in 2008—cocktails just don't get much better than the ones served here. Kimball House in Decatur, however, offers up classically inspired cocktails and plenty of absinthe in a sexy, modern environ we can't get enough of. The Sound Table's cocktail menu is constantly changing, and we've yet to have anything that disappoints. The historic and swanky Georgian Terrace Hotel in Midtown is home to the laidback Proof & Provision where they serve up stiff drinks and awesome food—you'll find the entrance to P&P on Ponce de Leon. And if you want to hit a bar to get in some of the city's best people watching, head to either Chops Lobster Bar or the St. Regis Bar in Buckhead—you won't be disappointed.

Chops Lobster Bar
70 West Paces Ferry Road, 404-262-2675,
www.buckheadrestaurants.com

Holeman & Finch Public House
2277 Peachtree Road, 404-948-1175,
www.holeman-finch.com

Kimball House
303 East Howard Avenue 404-378-3502, www.
kimball-house.com
Proof & Provision
659 Peachtree Street, 404-897-5045,
www.proofandprovision.com

The Sound Table
483 Edgewood Avenue, 404-835-2534,
www.thesoundtable.com

The St. Regis Bar
88 West Paces Ferry Road, 404-563-7900,
www.stregisatlanta.com/the-st-regis-bar

FEAST ON LOCAL FARE
AT THE ATLANTA FOOD TRUCK PARK

Forget about tracking the whereabouts of your favorite food truck. Hit the Atlanta Food Truck Park and there's a good chance it will be there. At any given time, ten of the city's most popular are parked here selling their goods, so you and nine of your BFFs can all dine on something different for dinner. It's BYOB, pet friendly, and there are plenty of tables and even green space to throw down a blanket and dine picnic style.

1850 Howell Mill Road, www.atlantafoodtruckpark.com
Neighborhood: Collier Hills

JOIN
A SUPPER CLUB

All the cool kids are doing it. But you're not so good at keeping up with e-mails or social media and always miss out on the fun. Check out the Atlanta Community Food Bank's (ACFB) Supper Club. You never have to be a "member." It's not about that. These dinners are about giving back to the food bank and eating delicious food, of course. You simply show up at the designated restaurant serving as that month's host and the restaurant will donate 20 percent of its proceeds to ACFB. No scrambling to sign up via last-minute e-mails. No secret locations. No cryptic menus. Just a monthly supper club for a great cause.

404-892-3333, www.acfb.org

STUFF YOUR FACE
AT THE ATLANTA FOOD & WINE FESTIVAL

The Atlanta Food & Wine Festival (AFWF) may still be in its infancy (it debuted in 2010), but its first few years on the food scene were pretty darn impressive. You never know what to expect from its culinary creators. You could find yourself lost on a fried chicken "trail" or end up tailgating Southern style at a soiree at JCT. Kitchen, one of Atlanta's best restaurants. Culinary classes and seminars teach everything you could ever want to know about wine, oysters, bacon, and booze. Just get your mind out of learning mode long enough to hit the Tasting Tents to sample bites and sip brews from some of the South's best restaurants and bartenders. At the end the day, kick your feet up at the Connoisseur Lounge, because if there's one thing you can be sure of at the AFWF, you'll finish it in full-on food coma.

www.atlfoodandwinefestival.com

EAT YOUR WAY
THROUGH KROG STREET MARKET

Gourmands are going mad for the goods at Krog Street Market. The refurbished warehouse space is home to a variety of retail markets, specialty food stores, and restaurants. Local chefs (Ford Fry, Eli Kirshtein, Todd Ginsberg, and Kevin Maxey) all have sit-down spots, but if you're more in the mood for a quick bite, you can grab something from one of the market stalls—the Spotted Trotter, Little Tart, Jeni's Ice Cream, Gu's Dumplings, and Grand Champion BBQ all have spots in this hip mixed-use development located right on the BeltLine.

99 Krog Street, www.krogstreetmarket.com
Neighborhood: Inman Park

BEER ME
AT SWEETWATER BREWERY

Grab a few of your closest friends, $10, and go sample some of Atlanta's own beer at the SweetWater Brewery tour. Nothing is too fancy here—it's more about socializing and sampling than anything (you get six tasting tickets and a souvenir glass). Don't lose sight of the goal though: There are typically about five chances to go behind the scenes, and you definitely don't want to miss the story about how a few college roommates from Colorado turned their passion for beer into Atlanta's most recognized brew. Tours are held Wednesday through Friday from 5:30 to 7:30 p.m.; Saturday and Sunday from 2:30 to 4:30 p.m.

195 Ottley Drive, 404-691-2537, www.sweetwaterbrew.com
Neighborhood: Midtown

Other awesome breweries to check out.

Blue Tarp Brewing Co.
731 East College Avenue, Decatur,
www.bluetarpbrew.com

Monday Night Brewing Company
670 Trabert Avenue, www.mondaynightbrewing.com

Red Hare Brewing Company
1998 Delk Industrial Boulevard, Marietta,
www.redharebrewing.com

Three Taverns Brewery
121 New Street,
www.threetavernsbrewery.com

Wild Heaven Craft Beers
135 Maple Street, Decatur,
www.wildheavencraftbeers.com

EAT HOT DOUGHNUTS
AT KRISPY KREME

There's just nothing like a hot Krispy Kreme glazed doughnut. Before you know it, you've lost all self-control and scarfed down a half dozen of the things. Go ahead and blame it on that neon sign that has blazed on Ponce de Leon in Midtown since 1965: Hot Krispy Kreme Doughnuts Now. I mean really. How can one be expected to resist that?

295 Ponce de Leon Avenue, 404-876-7307, www.krispykreme.com
Neighborhood: Midtown

HIT THE FOOD HALL
AT PONCE CITY MARKET

Ponce City Market is a massive warehouse reuse project that feature tons of dining options in its Food Hall from some of the South's best chefs, including James Beard Award-winners Anne Quatrano, Linton Hopkins and Sean Brock. You can grab a Latin-inspired sandwich at El Super Pan, one of the famed cheeseburgers at H&F Burger or fish tacos at Minero. If you're in the mood for South African wines, cheese and charcuterie, pull up a seat at Biltong Bar. For a little '60s glam, hit The Mercury—if the killer cocktails don't take you back, the stunning space will. There are also plenty of options for sweet treats—our faves are the Collier Candy Company and Honeysuckle Gelato.

675 Ponce de Leon Drive, 404-900-7900, www.poncecitymarket.com
Neighborhood: Poncey-Highland

TIP
Ponce City Market sits right on the Eastside Trail of the BeltLine. On a pretty day you start with a beer at Tap on Ponce and then walk the Eastside Trail all the way to Krog Street Market and enjoy dinner at any of the spots we listed on page 9.

WATCH THE SUN SET
FROM THE SUN DIAL

Hold onto your seats because the best way to get to the Sun Dial Restaurant at the top of the Westin Peachtree Plaza hotel is to take the eighty-five-second ride up one of the two outdoor glass elevators. But that ride isn't even where you'll get the best look at the city. Once you're inside the three-story restaurant, you'll overlook 360-degree views of the skyline no matter where you sit because this restaurant revolves. No need to worry about getting the spins—you will barely notice any movement; it takes nearly an hour for the restaurant to make a complete revolution. What will grab your attention is the constantly changing skyline outside the massive, three-story windows. Make a reservation early enough to watch the sun set—it's hard to beat from seventy-three stories above Peachtree.

210 Peachtree Street, 404-589-7506, www.sundialrestaurant.com
Neighborhood: Downtown

CELEBRATE ANYTHING
AT THE RITZ-CARLTON, BUCKHEAD

Atlantans love to brunch, and nobody does it quite like The Ritz-Carlton, Buckhead. The wildly popular buffet is offered only on Sundays—we imagine it's to give the chefs time to prepare all the food. Start out with a champagne cocktail from the Bubble Bar; we are partial to a handcrafted Bellini or Kir. Don't plan on eating anything else all day because multiple carving stations, several seafood options, caviar and all the trimmings, salads, a decadent cheese tray, charcuterie, fruit, antipasti, fresh bread, Belgian waffles, and traditional breakfast items don't even cover half of what's offered here. When it comes time for dessert, the options are mind blowing. You'll have to pick from about fifteen different sweets from the chefs' incredible selection.

3434 Peachtree Road, 404-237-2700, www.ritzcarlton.com/buckhead
Neighborhood: Buckhead

SCREAM
FOR ICE CREAM

A chocolate chip cone from Baskin-Robbins just isn't going to cut it for fans of ice cream in the ATL. That's OK—because the city is home to some stellar spots serving up scoops that will put just about any other ice cream to shame. High Road Craft has been a household name since opening in 2010 because of its bold flavors like mango chile lime sorbet and Aztec chocolate and caramel. You can have your beer and ice cream, too, with flavors like peach Lambic, honey IPA, and malted milk chocolate stout from Frozen Pints. Hit Jeni's Splendid Ice Creams for distinctive flavors like pistachio and honey, salty caramel, and black coffee. Morelli's creates new flavors like coconut ginger, Guinness gingersnap, and salted caramel every week. And if you have a hankering for gelato, head to Paolo's, where they've been making some of the best in the city since 1999.

Frozen Pints
Multiple locations, www.frozenpints.com

High Road Craft Ice Cream
678-701-7623,
www.highroadcraft.com

Jeni's Splendid Ice Creams
Multiple locations,
www.jenis.com

Morelli's Gourmet Ice Cream
Multiple locations,
www.morellisicecream.com

Paolo's Gelato
1025 Virginia Avenue, 404-607-0055,
www.paolosgelato.com

DINE OUT AND DO GOOD
AT STAPLEHOUSE

Chef Ryan Smith and Jen Hidinger are pushing the boundaries of culinary arts at the 2016 James Beard Award-nominated Staplehouse. The restaurant is a stone's throw from the childhood home of Martin Luther King Jr. in the ground floor of a renovated 115-year-old building. And while the simple architecture and history of the space is definitely part of the draw, it's way more than just the building's character that makes dining here so special. Smith's seasonal à la carte and five-course tasting menus (you purchase advance tickets for the tasting menu) rival any five-star restaurant in the country. But you'll enjoy it more knowing the money you spend at Staplehouse goes to The Giving Kitchen, a nonprofit that provides emergency assistance to Atlanta restaurant workers. The Giving Kitchen started after the late chef Ryan Hidinger was diagnosed with stage IV gall bladder cancer in 2102. The restaurant community rallied around Hidinger and his wife Jen, and raised more than $275,000 for his medical care, inspiring the couple to launch the organization before his death in 2014. Staplehouse, and The Giving Kitchen, now stands as a symbol of Atlanta's generous hospitality community.

541 Edgewood Avenue, 404-524-5005, www.staplehouse.com
Neighborhood: Old Fourth Ward

ENTER THE ATLANTA
CHILI COOK-OFF

We're not sure what gets more attention here—the chili or the contestants. Of course that's probably why your weekend recipe might actually have a chance of taking home a prize at this insane fall festival. The most important thing (after perfecting your exact concoction of beans, seasonings, and meat) is picking your team's name, and the more ridiculous the better—think the Stew-pids, Trailer Trash, and CUI (Cooking Under the Influence). Costumes and outlandish tent decor mandatory. (Not really, but, well, really.) This is the South, y'all.

www.theatlantachilicookoff.com

DRINK GOOD BEER
AT THE BRICK STORE PUB

It's been named one of the best beer lists in the world—and more than once. The Brick Store Pub is a neighborhood watering hole where you can go to enjoy dinner and a few brews, but you'd be selling yourself short. People go here to drink good beer. Just be prepared to painstakingly peruse the beer list—it's massive, with close to twenty rotating draught and seventy-five bottled beers, and that's just at the main bar downstairs. Be cautious at the upstairs Belgian Beer Bar, though. Eight additional rotating draughts and more than 120 Belgian/Belgian-style bottled beers are some of the best they serve, and many are high gravity meaning they contain a lot of alcohol—some as much as 14 percent by volume. Drink a couple of pints of Chimay Blue and you might not remember your name. I've seen it happen!

125 East Court Square, 404-687-0990, www.brickstorepub.com
Neighborhood: Decatur

TIP
If there's one bar in the ATL that gives the Brick Store Pub a run for its money it's the Porter Beer Bar in Little Five Points. The food here is fantastic, and the cocktails are always served strong. But it's the Porter's stellar 800-plus beer selection that makes this the spot for beer aficionados.
www.theporterbeerbar.com

TAKE A WORLD TOUR
ALONG BUFORD HIGHWAY

While we may not have our own Chinatown or Little Italy, what we do have in Atlanta is Buford Highway. The seven-lane highway essentially begins at Lenox and stretches for miles through what's been dubbed the "international corridor." And what you'll find along this route is some of the most authentic Chinese, Mexican, Vietnamese, Indian, Ethiopian, Cuban, and Korean food anywhere in the city.

COMER EN
NUEVO LAREDO CANTINA

Go for the chicken mole. Or Mexican barbecue brisket. Or lobster tacos. Or chips and salsa. Or margaritas. Just go and order anything because, yes, Nuevo Laredo really is as good as you've heard.

1495 Chattahoochee Avenue, 404-352-9009,
www.nuevolaredocantina.com
Neighborhood: The Westside

PORK UP
AT BACONFEST

Beer, bands, and bacon. What more do you need? Bottomless bacon? Got that, too. Aside from being a crazy porkapalooza (yep, I said it), BaconFest is a fund-raiser for Dad's Garage Improv Theatre, so even if you can't eat your weight in swine, at least you can spend your cash helping the funny fellows at Inman Park who always make you laugh. And anyway, we know you can eat your weight in swine—who do you think you are kidding?

www.baconfestatl.com
Neighborhood: Old Fourth Ward

PRAISE
SOUTHERN FOOD

Atlanta is a food lover's utopia. You can dine on cuisine from all types of cultures, and that's a mighty fine thing. Southern cuisine has also soared in popularity outside of the region, which validates a form of cooking that truly nourishes the soul. We are proud that our mothers' mothers' mothers are the ones who helped create it and equally pleased that our city's best chefs have perfected it. So missing a meal at one of these establishments would be like skipping out on Sunday supper at your momma's. You just don't do that, y'all.

Busy Bee
810 Martin Luther King Jr. Drive, 404-525-9212,
www.thebusybeecafe.com

Cakes & Ale
155 Sycamore Street, 404-377-7994,
www.cakesandalerestaurant.com

Empire State South
999 Peachtree Street, 404-541-1105,
www.empirestatesouth.com

Home Grown Ga.,
968 Memorial Drive, 404-222-0455,
www.homegrownga.com

JCT. Kitchen & Bar
1198 Howell Mill Road, 404-355-2252,
www.jctkitchen.com

Miller Union
999 Brady Avenue, 678-733-8550,
www.millerunion.com

FEAST ON
FRIED CHICKEN

We love to fry things in the South. Name a food and we have probably fried it—or at least tried. Of all the foods we have fried, there's nothing more quintessentially Southern than fried chicken, and it's serious business in this town. Battles are fought over what chef serves the best.

Any chef worth his or her salt knows good fried chicken must be brown and crispy on the outside and juicy on the inside—a tough feat to achieve when cooking to order. But there are a few who have it down to a science: Chef Zeb Stevenson of Watershed has carried on the restaurant's legendary fried chicken night spearheaded by original chef Scott Peacock. The only change is that it's now available for lunch and dinner on Wednesdays instead of Tuesdays. Buttermilk Kitchen chef and owner Suzanne Vizethann opens up her breakfast and lunch spot once a month for sellout Pop-Up Fried Chicken Suppers. Chef Shaun Doty serves fried chicken mild, Buffalo style, and hot (as hell) at his popular Chick-a-Biddy. Regulars at Table & Main would likely revolt if executive chef Ted Lahey took his fried chicken off the menu, as would diners at the Colonnade and South City Kitchen.

Buttermilk Kitchen
4225 Roswell Road, 678-732-3274,
www.buttermilkkitchen.com

Chick-a-Biddy
264 19th Street, 404-588-1888,
www.chickabiddyatl.com

South City Kitchen
Multiple locations
www.southcitykitchen.com

Table & Main
1028 Canton Street, Roswell, 678-869-5178,
www.tableandmain.com

The Colonnade
1879 Cheshire Bridge Road, 404-874-5642,
www.colonnadeatl.com

Watershed on Peachtree
1820 Peachtree Road, 404-809-3561,
www.watershedrestaurant.com

PIG OUT
ON BARBECUE

Deciding who has the best barbecue in Atlanta is just a silly game. You might like beef, and I might like pork. You might like a mustard- or tomato-based sauce while I prefer vinegar. Herein lies our problem: In Atlanta, it's really a mashup of all kinds of barbecue—a little bit of the Carolinas, Texas, Kansas City, and even Korean-style thrown in for good measure. That means there are as many styles of barbecue here as there are streets named Peachtree. So rather than trying to choose which is best, I say pig out on all of it. There's no harm in that, right?

Community Q BBQ
1361 Clairmont Road, Decatur, 404-633-2080,
www.communityqbbq.com

Daddy D'z BBQ Joynt
264 Memorial Drive, 404-222-0206,
www.daddydz.com

Dave Poe's
660 Whitlock Avenue, Marietta, 770-792-2272,
www.davepoes.com

Fox Bros. BBQ
1238 DeKalb Avenue, 404-577-4030,
www.foxbrosbbq.com

Grand Champion BBQ
Multiple locations
www.gcbbq.net

Heirloom Market BBQ
2243 Akers Mill Road, 770-612-2502,
www.heirloommarketbbq.com

Pig 'n' Chik
Multiple locations
www.pignchik.net

Sam's BBQ1
Multiple locations
www.bbq1.net

Swallow at the Hollow
1072 Green Street, Roswell, 678-352-1975,
www.swallowatthehollow.com

MUSIC AND ENTERTAINMENT

PULL SOME STRINGS
AT THE CENTER FOR PUPPETRY ARTS

Let your kids' imaginations soar with an outing to the Center for Puppetry Arts. Here they can enjoy magical puppetry performances, explore the museum's collection of marionettes, and even create their own puppets during fun interactive workshops and classes. Kids will love seeing Big Bird, several of Jim Henson's Muppets, and other incredible puppets, and parents can check out the Xperimental Puppetry Theater (XPT) shows— they're for the eighteen and over crowd and are put on by artists experimenting in puppetry, so expect the unexpected.

1404 Spring Street, 404-873-3391, www.puppet.org
Neighborhood: Midtown

PEEK AT THE PANDAS
AT ZOO ATLANTA

No doubt you'll agree that Lun Lun and Yang Yang are the cutest couple in all of Atlanta. Watching these cuddly black-and-white bears tumble and cavort, devour bamboo, and even doze off is pretty spectacular. But to stand side by side with one of them (or their cubs!) separated only by glass is something you'll never forget. During their time in Zoo Atlanta's Arthur M. Blank Family Foundation Giant Panda Conservation Center, Lun Lun has given birth to five cubs, including twins Mei Lun (may loon) and Mei Huan (may hwaan), born in July 2013—the first set to ever survive in the United States. Considering that experts deem the giant panda critically endangered, with perhaps just 1,600 left in the wild, we're pretty proud of what our pair is doing to ensure the panda's survival.

800 Cherokee Avenue, 404-624-9453, www.zooatlanta.org
Neighborhood: Grant Park

SET SAIL
WITH YACHT ROCK REVUE

Pull out your polyester pants and cheap sunglasses, because it's always smooth sailing when Yacht Rock Revue is onstage. This kitschy (we mean that in a good way) tribute band gets you grooving to some of the best (worst) light rock songs from the '70s you tried to forget that you once loved. The band's killer performances of hits like Hall & Oates's "Rich Girl," Paul McCartney and Wings's "Silly Love Songs," and "Africa" by Toto (a definite fan fave) are uncanny, but it's YRR's total originality and all-out antics that will have you on board for life.

www.pleaserock.com

TIP

Diehard fans of Yacht Rock can catch the band now more than ever at Venkman's restaurant and live music venue the heart of the Old Fourth Ward. That's because Venkman's features live music curated by partners/owners Peter Olson and Nicholas Niespodziani—the frontmen behind the popular band. Live musical acts play nearly every night, with special performances from Yacht Rock Revue regularly.

740 Ralph McGill Boulevard,
470-225-6162, www.venkmans.com

BE WOWED
BY THE ATLANTA SYMPHONY ORCHESTRA

Atlanta is lucky to have a world-class orchestra right in its own backyard. Renowned maestro Robert Spano has led the Atlanta Symphony Orchestra to six Grammy Awards and boosted its reputation internationally. Still haven't purchased tickets? Perhaps you should rethink the idea of what it means to see the ASO at one of its Pops series concerts. You can experience classical music and contemporary hits set to flying aerialists and acrobatic talent at Cirque de la Symphonie, or hear the ASO's take on the music of the Beatles, David Bowie, Carole King, Elton John, and more. Trust me, this isn't always your momma's symphony.

1280 Peachtree Street, 404-733-4900, www.atlantasymphony.org
Neighborhood: Midtown

GO RETRO
AT THE STARLIGHT DRIVE-IN THEATRE

Pack up the kids and the car and park it for a movie night they'll not soon forget. The Starlight Drive-In has been part of Atlanta since 1949, and by the looks of it, not much has changed since then. Everything is totally 1950s vintage, and with six screens, there's almost always a family-friendly film playing. Bonus: You can pack a picnic and "tailgate" before the movie to avoid spending an arm and leg on popcorn, sodas, and candy.

2000 Moreland Avenue, 404-627-5786, www.starlightdrivein.com
Neighborhood: East Atlanta

TIP
Gates open two hours before showtime, and the lines can get long, so plan on being there early to get a good parking spot—and to let the kids play off some of their energy before the movie starts.

FEEL THE BLUES
AT NORTHSIDE TAVERN

It doesn't get much grittier than Atlanta's Northside Tavern. This smoky dive on the Westside screams the blues and has been cranking out the city's best for more than forty years. Danny "Mudcat" Dudeck is a local legend who lays down his bayou-baked tunes weekly and captivates the Northside Tavern barflies faster than they can order up another bourbon on the rocks. Live blues, jazz, zydeco, and soul music wail from these walls seven days a week, so when you need a place in town to soothe your soul or drown your sorrows, you do it here.

1058 Howell Mill Road, 404-874-8745, www.northsidetavern.com
Neighborhood: Downtown

SKATE
WITH THE ATLANTA ROLLERGIRLS

Roller-skating with the girls just isn't what it used to be. No more white skates with pink wheels. No more furry skate pom-poms to make the other girls jealous. Not these days. Oh, today's girls are still vicious just like we (thought we) were, but now instead of fluffy accessories and schoolgirl antics, these chicks fight with full-on brute force and elbow pads. Teams of tough girls with names like the Apocalypstix, Denim Demons, Sake Tuyas, and Toxic Shocks battle it out on the rink (literally) for a championship trophy. Go cheer them on, because these ladies are hard core when it comes to roller derby—and they're a blast to watch.

400 Ponce de Leon Avenue, www.atlantarollergirls.com
Neighborhood: Midtown

CHANNEL THE DEAD
ON A ZOMBIE TOUR

OK, not really. But since Atlanta's pretty much known as the Hollywood of the South these days, you'll at least see the spots where the zombies from The *Walking Dead reign.* The Big Zombie Tour Part One runs on Saturdays between Memorial and Labor days and takes you to spots from the hit show like the abandoned hospital where Sheriff Grimes awoke to find the world overrun by walkers. The Big Zombie Tour Part Two heads south to Woodbury, I mean Senoia, where you'll see the Governor's Mansion, Oaks Motor Inn, and the old feed building. I'm getting scared just thinking about it.

www.atlantamovietours.com

GO BIG HAIR BAND
AT METALSOME

Imagine you. Onstage. With a live heavy metal band. No, we're not talking stadium tour just yet, but at the 10 High, you can pretty much channel your favorite big hair band front man during Metalsome Live Band Karaoke night. It's first come, first served, so if you want to impress with your best rendition of Mötley Crüe's "Dr. Feelgood," you better get here early.

816 North Highland Avenue, 404-873-3607, www.10highclub.com
Neighborhood: Virginia Highland

TIP

If metal isn't quite your thing,
check out the always-ridiculous
Wednesday night Church Organ Karaoke
at Sister Louisa's Church of the Living Room and
Ping Pong Emporium. You'll don a church choir
robe and belt out classic songs to the unforgettable
sounds of an organ—all from behind the pulpit.

466 Edgewood Avenue, 404-522-8275,
www.sisterlouisaschurch.com

SEE A SHOW
AT EDDIE'S ATTIC

If you want to hear live music in the ATL, head to Eddie's Attic in Decatur, where the famed "listening room" has helped launch the careers of several major musicians, including John Mayer, Sugarland, Shawn Mullins, and Josh Joplin. Other big names like Sheryl Crow, Brandi Carlile, and the Black Crowes have also played gigs here.

515-B North McDonough Street, 404-377-4976, www.eddiesattic.com
Neighborhood: Decatur

More Spots to See Live Shows

Red Clay Theatre
Eddie Owen's 260-seat listening room is
where you can hear some of the country's best
singer-songwriters—think Holly Williams,
Matthew Perryman Jones,
and Francine Reed.
3116 Main Street, Duluth, 678-892-6373,
www.eddieowenpresents.com

Smith's Olde Bar
Smith's has always been the place to hear the next big
band in the ATL.
1578 Piedmont Road, 404-875-1522,
www.smithsoldebar.com

The EARL
Local and indie bands are the mainstay at this gritty
East Atlanta restaurant and lounge.
488 Flat Shoals Avenue, 404-522-3950,
www.badearl.com

The Goat Farm Arts Center
This twelve-acre arts studio sits among the ruins
of factory buildings and hosts indie bands and
experiment musical acts.
Foster Street NW

Variety Playhouse
This combo theater/nightclub in quirky Little Five
Points is a preferred venue of indie acts like Neko Case,
Neutral Milk Hotel, and local fave Yacht Rock Revue.
1099 Euclid Avenue, 404-524-7354,
www.varietyplayhouse.com

GET HIGH
ON SKYVIEW

It may not be the London Eye, but the SkyView Ferris wheel in the Luckie-Marietta District is still pretty impressive. It's a whopping twenty stories tall with forty-two temp-controlled gondolas, and from the top you get a pretty unbeatable view of the Atlanta skyline. Bypass the lines and opt for the VIP experience. These swanky gondolas feature Ferrari leather seats, champagne, a TV, and glass floors so you can look straight down from 200 feet above.

168 Luckie Street, 828-318-3639, www.skyviewatlanta.com
Neighborhood: Downtown

FREAK OUT
AT NETHERWORLD

There are haunted houses and then there is Netherworld. If you haven't been freaked out at this nightly Halloween fright fest, don't let another October pass by without getting the, well, you-know-what scared out of you. For years people have been screaming over the Hollywood-quality creations, intense sets, and elaborate special effects from chief makeup artists Bill "Splat" Johnson and Roy Wooley. And if you can keep your eyes open while you're finding your way through the dark, spooky mazes, keep them peeled for sets from horror flicks like Zombieland, Van Helsing, and Prisoners. Just leave your cowardly friends at home.

6624 Dawson Boulevard, 404-608-2484, www.fearworld.com
Neighborhood: Norcross

USHER IN SPRING
AT THE DOGWOOD FESTIVAL

Aside from that layer of yellow pollen coating anything and everything, not much signals spring in Atlanta like the Dogwood Festival. It's been a city staple for more than seventy-five years. Spring just hasn't sprung until the kids scarf down funnel cakes, then bounce off their sugar high in the huge inflatables. You, on the other hand, can take in the warm spring air at the artists' market, food and wine tastings, and at the disc dog competitions, then wind down your weekend under the stars listening to live music.

Piedmont Park, 404-817-6642, www.dogwood.org
Neighborhood: Midtown

Atlanta is known for hosting a wide range of festivals throughout the year. These are some of the best!

The nonprofit, independent AJC Decatur Book Festival is the country's largest and hosts hundreds of authors during Labor Day weekend for book signings, poetry slams, and writing workshops.
www.decaturbookfestival.com

Every spring, the Atlanta Film Festival screens some of the country's best independent films (and has for more than forty years) in genres ranging from sci-fi and horror to documentaries and animation.
www.atlantafilmfestival.com

Chef Ford Fry's summer Attack of the Killer Tomato Festival pits chefs and mixologists against one another to see who can concoct the best tasting treat using, what else, tomatoes.
http://www.killertomatofest.com

The National Black Arts Festival is held in the fall and is the world's largest celebration of dance, film, music, theater, and visual arts by artists of African descent.
www.nbaf.org

Taste of Atlanta is the foodie's fall festival where the city's top restaurants and chefs dish out their best creations.
www.tasteofatlanta.com

GEEK OUT
AT THE DRAGON CON PARADE

Sure, it's a convention for sci-fi and fantasy, comic books, and gaming, but everyone knows you really go for the parade. When else do you get the chance to see Stormtroopers and Supermans, Ghostbusters and Trekkies, comic book heroes and villains, marching down Peachtree Street? Trust me when I say this display of world-class costumes puts anything you've ever seen on Halloween to shame.

www.dragoncon.org
Neighborhood: Downtown

Other Awesome Atlanta Parades

Inman Park Parade
The Inman Park Festival falls the last weekend in April
and includes the quirkiest street parade around.
www.inmanparkfestival.org

Little Five Points Halloween Parade
This killer parade starts promptly at 4 p.m. and brings
out some of the wildest Halloween wear in the country.
www.l5phalloween.com

Pride Parade
The South's largest three-day Pride Festival in October
culminates with the Pride Parade down Peachtree Street,
where thousands of spectators join in to cheer on the
LBGT community.
www.atlantapride.org

St. Patrick's Day Parade
This annual parade celebrating everything Irish has
featured dancers, musicians, floats, and marching bands
for more than a hundred years.
www.stpatsparadeatlanta.com

GET DAZED
AT THE ATLANTA BOTANICAL GARDEN

The Fuqua Orchid Center's collection of intoxicating orchids is unlike any other in the United States—it's mesmerizing no matter what time of the year you see it. But make a point to visit during the annual Orchid Daze exhibition and you'll see the garden's rarest and most delicate orchids displayed artistically and thematically. Past exhibitions have incorporated surreal art, colors, and even sculptures by Hans Godo Fräbel.

1345 Piedmont Avenue, 404-876-5859, www.atlantabotanicalgarden.org
Neighborhood: Midtown

ROCK OUT
AT BIG MIKE GEIER'S ELVIS ROYALE

The always show-stopping Big Mike Geier, his thirteen-piece Kingsized Rock 'n' Roll Orchestra, and the sexy Dames Aflame Showgirls put on quite a spectacle at this show celebrating all things Elvis Presley. It's held twice a year—to honor the rock-and-roll legend's birthday in January and his death in August. Don your best Elvis jumpsuit to march onstage during the Cavalcade of Elvis, or just go as you are and tell your friends who stayed home you swear you spotted the King in Little Five Points. Technically, it's not a lie.

www.elvisroyale.com

GET FUNKY
AT THE ATLANTA JAZZ FESTIVAL

Thirty days of jazz hit the city every May for what's considered to be one of the country's best jazz festivals this side of NOLA. You'll be able to groove to some of the genre's best upcoming artists throughout the month at intimate performances across town. Then end the month-long celebration with a party-packed weekend of live shows with your besties at Piedmont Park's three-day outdoor concert Memorial Day weekend.

www.atlantafestivals.com
Neighborhood: Midtown

SWIM WITH WHALE SHARKS
AT THE GEORGIA AQUARIUM

And manta rays. And giant grouper. And Southern stingrays. The 6.3-million-gallon Ocean Voyager exhibit is where you can suit up and either scuba or snorkel among some of the aquarium's most famous fish—and it's the only place in the world where you're guaranteed to swim with massive whale sharks. If that's just too close for your comfort, wade in waist high for a hands-on experience with the enchanting Beluga whales. You'll interact with and even get to feed the animals alongside their trainers. Kids also can participate in exciting encounters with dolphins, sea otters, and penguins or host their own sleepover to explore exhibits after hours. But there's nothing wrong with just taking a day to explore the entire aquarium the good old-fashioned way.

225 Baker Street, 404-581-4000, www.georgiaaquarium.org
Neighborhood: Downtown

WALK ON THE WILD SIDE
AT NOAH'S ARK ANIMAL SANCTUARY

Lions and tigers and bears, oh my! At Noah's Ark Animal Sanctuary in Locust Grove, they live together in harmony. The 250-acre sanctuary's most famous residents are, in fact, a 1,000-pound American black bear named Baloo, a 350-pound Bengal tiger known as Shere Khan, and a 350-pound African lion named Leo that were all rescued as cubs during a 2001 drug raid in Atlanta. The three, affectionately known as BLT, have lived together ever since, completely clueless that they, well, shouldn't. Noah's Ark takes in other injured or abandoned animals and provides them with rehabilitation, training, and suitable habitats. You can visit them while you walk the miles of nature trails, where you might cross paths with free-roaming llamas or see monkeys swinging from the vines. Your kids can get up close and personal with the goats, rabbits, and ducks in the Ark's petting zoo.

712 LG Griffin Road, Locust Grove, 770-957-0888,
www.noahs-ark.org

LET THE MUSIC PLAY
AT MUSIC MIDTOWN

Music fans simply can't miss this three-day party held annually at Piedmont Park. It draws big crowds and even bigger bands—everyone from Pearl Jam, Red Hot Chili Peppers, and Ludacris have graced the stages, and every year festival producers manage to improve the lineup. Now if we can only get Mother Nature to cooperate from year to year as well, Music Midtown would be the must-attend event in Atlanta, hands down.

www.musicmidtown.com
Neighborhood: Midtown

TWIST AND SHOUT
AT JOHNNY'S HIDEAWAY

It may be cheesy and even a little sleazy. (The servers wear T-shirts that say "Got Cougar?" for god's sake.) But neither the owners nor the clientele seems to be ashamed of that. There's just something about Johnny's Hideaway that makes it one hell of a night out on the town, no matter what age you are—or what age person you might be looking to meet. DJs here play everything from Elvis to Earth, Wind & Fire, so getting your groove on is easy, as long as you're fine sharing the dance floor with, ahem, kids of all ages.

3771 Roswell Road, 404-233-8026, www.johnnyshideaway.com
Neighborhood: Buckhead

DO SOME SOUL SEARCHING
ON THE ROSWELL GHOST TOUR

You might have to sleep with your light on after this two-hour supernatural tour through the historic City of Roswell. Guides lead the "soul-searching" masses through a walking tour filled with unexplainable activities and historical info on Roswell. The outing hits pre–Civil War Bulloch Hall, Barrington Hall, the Founders' Cemetery, the "creepy house," and, of course, the historic Roswell Mill, which produced material used for Confederate Army uniforms during the Civil War. For that, General Sherman had the mill destroyed and charged all mill workers (mostly women and children) with treason and shipped them north to prison camps. Ghost Tour owner and paranormal investigator Dianna Avena thinks many of Roswell's supernatural residences are displaced mill workers trying to reconnect with loved ones in the afterlife. Spooky!

770-649-9922, www.roswellghosttour.com
Neighborhood: Roswell

DANCE WITH DINOSAURS
AT MARTINIS & IMAX

Picture this: You have a stiff martini in your hand, live jazz tunes are playing in the background, and there's a forty-seven-foot Giganotosaurus towering above you. Sounds like just another night at Fernbank's Martinis & IMAX. The Museum of Natural History provides the ultimate backdrop for this Friday night tradition, which starts with a few cocktails and friends, then ends with the latest IMAX film on the biggest screen in town.

767 Clifton Road, 404-929-6300, www.fernbankmuseum.org
Neighborhood: Druid Hills

RAMBLE ON
AT THE WREN'S NEST

Story time will never be the same after you've spent a Saturday at the historic home of author Joel Chandler Harris listening to the famous African American folklore tales of Brer Rabbit the way they were meant to be heard—from the mouth of a gifted "Rambler." Storytellers like Akbar Imhotep, who has been here since 1985, will captivate you and your kids with renditions of tales like Brer Rabbit Takes a Ride, How Brer Coon Gets His Meat, and Brer Rabbit and the Tar Baby. Every Rambler has a style all his own, but they share one thing in common at these Saturday story sessions: a passion for all things Brer Rabbit.

1050 Ralph David Abernathy Boulevard, 404-753-7735,
www.wrensnest.org
Neighborhood: The West End

LOL
AT WHOLE WORLD IMPROV THEATRE

It's unscripted and unrehearsed and you drive the laughs. So grab a couch and be prepared for just about anything—and we do mean anything. Cast members and the emcee make sure that the audience guides the live improv performance, so don't be shy or you could become part of the show.

1216 Spring Street, 404-817-7529, www.wholeworldtheatre.com
Neighborhood: Midtown

SPORTS AND RECREATION

GET IN A GAME
AT THE TED

The Ted is the nickname for Turner Field, by the way. And considering that this former Olympic stadium will no longer be home to the Braves beginning with the 2017 baseball season, you'll want to get in a game or two before "America's Team" heads to their new home in Cobb County. Grab a few "cheap" seats, head to the ball field early, and snag a table at the Braves Chop House. Order a cold beer, a hot dog, and you're in the ideal spot overlooking center field—not to mention you have a full bar and wait staff at your disposal. Of course, home plate seats are great, but if a slugger hits one deep in your direction, get your hands on that ball fast because it's definitely going to be a keeper.

755 Hank Aaron Drive, www.atlantabraves.com
Neighborhood: Downtown

SUPPORT
YOUR ATL TEAMS

Atlanta has a reputation for having fair-weather fans. We couldn't even keep our NHL Thrashers in town and all but sent them packing to colder Canadian climes. But there's a cult fan base building for the ATL's minor league teams, and going to these games is quite an experience. The Gwinnett Gladiators play for the East Coast Hockey League, the minor league for the American Hockey League, and made the Kelly Cup Final in 2006, losing to the Alaska Aces. The Gwinnett Braves are the official Minor League team for the Atlanta Braves. These games pack a punch with players just a few at bats away from the big leagues. The Atlanta Silverbacks has both men's and women's teams that play in the North American Soccer League, which is the second tier of the American Soccer Pyramid. The games are fast and physical, and fans are rowdy and raucous. They light flares when the Silverbacks score and think nothing of heckling the other team, all in the name of good sport.

www.gwinnettgladiators.com,
www.milb.com,
www.atlantasilverbacks.com

REACH THE SUMMIT
OF STONE MOUNTAIN

Saying you hiked to the top of Stone Mountain may not seem like that big of a deal until you actually do it. It is, after all, one of the largest pieces of exposed granite in the world. Its north face carving of Confederate generals Stonewall Jackson, Jefferson Davis, and Robert E. Lee (he's as tall as a nine-story building!) also happens to be the world's largest. And once you reach the top after your climb—it does get a little steep and strenuous near the end—you're rewarded with sweeping views of the state. Some say you can see as far as sixty miles on a cold, clear day. Sure, there are those that wimp out and ride the Summit Skyride gondola to the top, but when you're surveying the Atlanta skyline in the distance, it looks a whole lot sweeter to you as you catch your breath.

1000 Robert E. Lee Boulevard, 770-498-5690,
www.stonemountainpark.com
Neighborhood: Stone Mountain

LIGHT UP
AT THE ATLANTA MOON RIDE

It's tough enough navigating Atlanta's streets on your bike by day. So good luck after the sun goes down—except during the Atlanta Moon Ride. This annual spring charity event for Bert's Big Adventure is when you're actually encouraged to hit the streets after dark for a wild and wacky 6.5-mile bike ride through the ATL. It's totally safe because the streets are closed to traffic, so bring the kids and bike by moonlight. Costumes encouraged!

www.atlantamoonride.com

RUN YOUR TAIL OFF
AT THE PEACHTREE ROAD RACE

If you've stuck to that New Year's resolution (and we know you have), join 60,000 of your best friends while you run your you-know-what off at the Peachtree Road Race. It's the world's largest party, I mean 10K, held every July 4, where a collective 34 million calories are burned. Or you can just walk it with the rest of us who simply do it for the coveted finisher's T-shirt.

www.peachtreeroadrace.org

SHOOT
THE HOOCH

By tube or raft or kayak or canoe. Just do it. You can thank me later.

Azalea Park, 770-650-1008,
www.shootthehooch.com
Neighborhood: Roswell

TAKE A TWIRL
AT THE ST. REGIS ATLANTA

The St. Regis Atlanta's 40,000-square-foot Pool Piazza provides quite the fairy-tale setting for your wintertime ice-skating adventure under the stars. The rink is covered in a canopy of sheer white fabric and twinkling white lights where you can channel your best Gracie Gold and glide and twirl to the sounds of holiday music. Warm up afterward by the outdoor fireplace with a hot toddy and s'mores.

88 West Paces Ferry Road, 404-563-7797, www.stregisatlanta.com
Neighborhood: Buckhead

GO FOR MILES
ON THE SILVER COMET TRAIL

Get out of the city on foot, by bike, on Rollerblades, or even on horseback on this sixty-mile paved trail that heads west of Atlanta. It's built on the old rail line of the Silver Comet passenger train and cuts through some spectacular natural scenery, traversing rivers, rocky cliffs, and lush greenery. At the Georgia–Alabama state line, the trail meets up with the thirty-three-mile Chief Ladiga Trail, creating nearly ninety-five miles of car-free paved trails from Smyrna to Anniston, Alabama. How's that for a day on the bike?

www.silvercometga.com,
www.pathfoundation.org

BIKE
THE BELTLINE

Park the car, pull out your two-wheeler, and tour some of Atlanta's best neighborhoods on the BeltLine. The miles of urban trails follow a historic rail line that once completely circled downtown Atlanta. The track is slowly being revitalized into urban hiking trails and parks that will eventually connect forty-five neighborhoods in the city.

Stick to the Eastside Trail (it's the first to be completed) to hit the Historic Fourth Ward Park and "drop in" on one of the bowls at the Old Fourth Ward Skatepark. Permanent and temporary public art installations line much of the trails, so there's always something cool to see, whether you're walking, biking, or running. And by all means, march with thousands in the BeltLine's annual Lantern Parade. This fun-filled procession lights up the Eastside Trail on the first Saturday after Labor Day in what's become one of Atlanta's most colorful parades.

404-446-4400, www.beltline.org

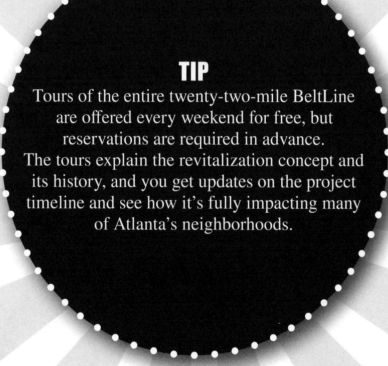

TIP

Tours of the entire twenty-two-mile BeltLine are offered every weekend for free, but reservations are required in advance. The tours explain the revitalization concept and its history, and you get updates on the project timeline and see how it's fully impacting many of Atlanta's neighborhoods.

SPLASH IN
THE FOUNTAIN OF RINGS
AT CENTENNIAL OLYMPIC PARK

Kids are encouraged to be, well, kids at Centennial Olympic
Park where they can skip and scamper through the Fountain of
Rings. On warm days, it comes alive with children soaked from
head to toe, whose parents have given up on keeping them dry.
No doubt the main attraction at the park since being built for
the 1996 Centennial Olympic Games, the fountain wows with
a show choreographed to different songs several times a day.
At night those Olympic Rings light up to the music, adding an
entirely different element to the atmosphere.

www.centennialpark.com
Neighborhood: Downtown

BECOME A RANGER
AT KENNESAW MOUNTAIN NATIONAL BATTLEFIELD PARK

Key battles of the Civil War were fought at this 2,900-acre expanse; trenches, earthworks, and even cannons still remain from the two-week clash that raged here. Today, the evidence is all part of the Kennesaw Mountain National Battlefield Park, and much of it sits along the eighteen miles of hiking trails or at the park museum where artifacts found on the site are on display. The park is popular for biking, jogging, and horseback riding, and kids who want to explore can become certified Junior Rangers (with a badge and certificate!) if they complete the fun tasks in the Junior Ranger Activity Book.

900 Kennesaw Mountain Drive, Kennesaw, 770-427-4686,
www.nps.gov/kemo
Neighborhood: Kennesaw

GO DEEP
AT THE SEC CHAMPIONSHIP GAME

Yes, there's college football all over the country, but in Atlanta, we have the SEC Championship. And everyone knows that the SEC is the toughest division in college ball. So in early December, if you want to watch two real football teams battle it out for bragging rights, you better get your tickets early because this is one title game that's always a sellout.

www.secdigitalnetwork.com
Neighborhood: Downtown

TIP

Hit the College Football Hall of Fame and get an up-close and personal look at the stories and achievements of the college players who have made the game what it is today. And while you're there, don't miss your chance to test your football skills in the Chick-fil-A Peach Bowl Skill Zone, where you can play every position from field goal kicker to quarterback.

250 Marietta Street, 404-880-4800, www.cfbhall.com

CLIMB HIGH
AT PANOLA MOUNTAIN STATE PARK

We don't know anywhere else that makes climbing trees, well, a sport. Some brilliant person at Panola Mountain State Park must have remembered how much fun it really is and decided to turn tree climbing into a safe and challenging adventure. You can scale "Naomi Ruth," the massive 100-foot Southern Red Oak in the park's main tree grove on an introductory climb or head deeper into the forest and tackle the canopy on a Wild Climb. There's even an overnight ZZZ's in the Trees program where you can sleep (or try to) in the trees. Where was this when I was a kid?

2600 Highway 155, Stockbridge, 770-389-7801,
www.gastateparks.org/treeclimbs

FLY LIKE A FALCON
AT BANNING MILLS

Ever wanted to just take off and soar above the trees like a majestic bird of prey? Surely you've at least dreamed of being able to fly. Historic Banning Mills just west of Atlanta is where you can go to make your dreams of flight come true. Just hop on its Flight of the Falcon where you're strapped in like Superman to "fly" along the 3,400-foot zip line just above the tree canopy and over Snake Creek Gorge. If that doesn't take your breath away, there are miles and miles of lines to zip down, including the Screaming Eagle, which, at 40,000 lineal feet, holds the Guinness World Record for the longest continuous zip line.

205 Horseshoe Dam Road, Banning, 770-834-9149,
www.historicbanningmills.com

UNLEASH YOUR PUPS
AT PIEDMONT PARK'S DOG PARK

It's OK to let the dogs out at Piedmont Park's dog park. In fact, you're encouraged to. The three-acre park is just one of a few places in the city where your furry friends can let it all out and run freely. The annual end-of-summer Splish Splash Doggie Bash (it opens the Piedmont Park Aquatic Center to pups and their humans for a fee) and other dog-related fund-raising events help pay for the park's maintenance and upkeep, so there's never a cover charge to get your pooch past the velvet ropes.

www.piedmontpark.org
Neighborhood: Midtown

CHILL OUT
AT CASCADE SPRINGS NATURE PRESERVE

You can get a glimpse into Atlanta's Civil War past all over this town. Sherman made sure of that. One now-serene place where you can see his scars is Cascade Springs where the Battle of Utoy Creek was fought in 1864. Many earthworks and rifle pits still remain, and several small natural springs continue to flow into the Utoy Creek with water that was once considered healing. The 120-plus-acre picturesque preserve is one of the oldest forests inside the city limits and is as peaceful as can be, despite its ties to Sherman's battle against Atlanta.

2851 Cascade Road, 404-546-6788
Neighborhood: Cascade Heights

TIP
Just two miles from the preserve is Atlanta's Historic Utoy Cemetery. It's located behind the old Utoy Primitive Church, which served as a field hospital during the Battle of Utoy Creek. Consequently, many of the soldiers who died in the battle are buried here.

1465 Cahaba Drive,
www.utoycemeteryinc.org

SEE THE GORGE IN ANOTHER LIGHT
ON A FULL-MOON SUSPENSION BRIDGE HIKE

When the calendar shows a full moon, head up to Tallulah Gorge State Park and prepare to take a nighttime hike. Park rangers lead you down the mile-and-a-half trail into the Tallulah Gorge, and the glow of the full moon provides all the light you'll need. (OK, you may want to take a flashlight.) Just be sure to pause and take in the sights and sounds of the waterfalls and river eighty feet below the suspension bridge—you'll see the gorge in completely differently light, literally.

338 Jane Hurt Yarn Drive, Tallulah Falls, 706-754-7981,
www.gastateparks.org/tallulahgorge

TREK THE TRAILS
AT SWEETWATER CREEK PARK

A leisurely hike on this popular park's Red Trail takes you to the ruins of the New Manchester mill and the rapids of Sweetwater Creek. Hop on the Blue Trail near the mill ruins for a quiet look at the park's wildflowers, ferns, shrubs, and trees. Reach the Yellow Trail just off the Red, where you'll come to a bridge that crosses Sweetwater Creek amid stunning hardwood forests. Check out White Trail for some of the most remote paths through the park, including trails up to Jack's Lake and the Jack's Hill area, a former farming community now known for its open meadows.

1750 Mt. Vernon Road, Lithia Springs, 770-732-5871,
www.gastateparks.org/sweetwatercreek

PUT THE PEDAL TO THE METAL
AT PETIT LE MANS

The world's fastest cars hit the track at Road Atlanta at this four-day world-class racing festival. Everyone is in awe watching top drivers battle it out in twelve races, including the thousand-mile endurance race. Kids will love the Petit Pit Stop's bouncy houses and face painting, and you'll love that they get in for free.

5300 Winder Highway, Braselton, 770-967-6143,
www.roadatlanta.com

TIP

If you can't make it to Petit Le Mans, Road Atlanta has an event going on just about every month for both car and motorcycle enthusiasts. It's also home to the Skip Barber Racing School where you can get behind the wheel of a Skip Barber Formula car and put the pedal to the metal on the Road Atlanta track yourself.

DRIVE A DESTROYER
AT TANK TOWN USA

You don't have to join the army to sit behind the controls of a 34,000-pound military tank. Just head to Blue Ridge and hand over $100 and you'll get ten full minutes to drive one of these massive vehicles around terrain that will send your heart to your throat in seconds. If you drop an extra $400, they'll give you twenty-five minutes at the wheel and even let you crush a car.

10408 Appalachian Highway, Morganton, 706-633-6072,
www.tanktownusa.com

TEE OFF
AT THE PGA TOUR CHAMPIONSHIP

When you're not playing golf on a September weekend, you might as well be watching it, right? In Atlanta it doesn't get much better than when the world's best battle it out at the East Lake Golf Club. It's home to the annual PGA Tour Championship where the winner walks away with a cool $1.5 million. Not too shabby for a few days on the greens.

2575 Alston Drive, www.pgatour.com
Neighborhood: East Lake

TAKE OFF
AT PEACHTREE-DEKALB AIRPORT PARK

The skies are always friendly at this charming airplane-theme playground. It's located right next to the runway at PDK airport, so if your kids aren't busy on the swing set and jungle gym, they'll certainly be wowed watching small planes and helicopters take off and land just yards away. When it's time for dinner, grab a burger at Downwind Restaurant next door.

2000 Airport Road, www.pdkairport.org
Neighborhood: Chamblee

CULTURE AND HISTORY

WALK IT OFF
AT CASTLEBERRY HILL ART STROLL

Art appreciation is easy when you can pop in and out of more than a dozen galleries in one of downtown's historic hoods, for free. Galleries like the Besharat Contemporary, Marcia Wood Gallery, and the Granite Room stay open late in Castleberry Hill on the second Friday of the month, making walking the streets of this funky warehouse district one of the coolest cultural gigs around.

www.castleberryhill.org
Neighborhood: Castleberry Hill

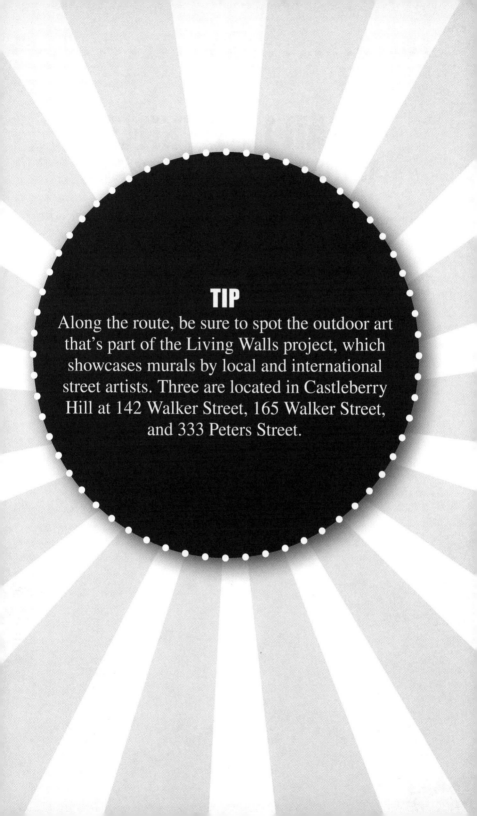

TIP

Along the route, be sure to spot the outdoor art that's part of the Living Walls project, which showcases murals by local and international street artists. Three are located in Castleberry Hill at 142 Walker Street, 165 Walker Street, and 333 Peters Street.

HEAR JAZZ TUNES
AT THE HIGH MUSEUM OF ART

Avoiding Friday afternoon rush hour never sounds as good as it does when you're tapping to the tunes of live jazz at the High Museum of Art. The wildly popular Friday Jazz combines live music, cocktails, and admission to all of the museum's current exhibits. The musicians are always stellar and wow the crowds—almost as much as the art. Almost.

1280 Peachtree Street, 404-733-4444, www.high.org
Neighborhood: Midtown

SEE THE CIVIL WAR
AT THE CYCLORAMA

We take our Civil War history seriously in Atlanta, and there's probably no more moving (literally and figuratively) memorial to the Battle of Atlanta than the Cyclorama. At 42 feet tall and 358 feet in circumference, it is said to be the largest painting in the world and depicts the July 22, 1864, battle—with three-dimensional figures and terrain, music, and narration—that eventually led to the fall of the Confederacy.

Atlanta History Center, 130 West Paces Ferry Road, 404-814-4000,
www.atlantahistorycenter.com
Neighborhood: Buckhead

TIP
A complete and full restoration on The Battle of Atlanta will begin at the painting's new home at the Atlanta History Center in late 2016. The restoration, which will return the massive cyclorama to its original hourglass shape, size, and height, will be open to the public in the new Lloyd and Mary Ann Whitaker Cyclorama Building and is expected to be completed in 2018.

DISCOVER OUR PAST
AT THE ATLANTA HISTORY CENTER

This gem of Atlanta culture is like a depository of our city's rich and diverse past. The entire center encompasses thirty-three acres in the heart of Buckhead and includes the iconic Swan House (what girl has not envisioned herself as a bride walking down those magnificent steps into its lush backyard gardens?), the Atlanta History Museum, the Smith Family Farm, six gardens, and the Kenan Research Center.

Civil War buffs can step back in time and tour the museum's Civil War and Military collections. It is home to at least one of every weapon and uniform used by both the Union and Confederate armies and is considered the world's best for a reason. The Urban History Collection showcases materials that reflect how Atlanta has developed and changed throughout history, and how outside influences continue to shape the city. Documents date back to the time of slavery right up to recent advances in Atlanta's LGBT community. Kids will love the Centennial Olympic Games Museum for its souvenir pins, flags, street banners, uniforms, medals, and costumes—all from the 1996 Atlanta games.

If you'd rather explore your Atlanta history outdoors, take the little ones to reimagine real life on the Civil War–era Piedmont Smith Family Farm. They can perform actual farm tasks or simply survey the 1840s plantation-style Tullie Smith House. It survived the Civil War and was moved from its original location nearby in the early '70s. Today, it is listed on the National Register of Historic Places.

130 West Paces Ferry Road, 404-814-4000,
www.atlantahistorycenter.com
Neighborhood: Buckhead

CELEBRATE THE DREAM
AT THE MARTIN LUTHER KING JR. NATIONAL HISTORIC SITE

Dr. Martin Luther King Jr.'s demand for civil rights in the '60s brought about profound changes in our country. His dream and legacy will forever remain part of Atlanta at the MLK National Historic Site, which includes his childhood home on Auburn Avenue, Ebenezer Baptist Church where he, his father, and his grandfather all preached, and the D.R.E.A.M. Gallery at the National Park Service Visitor Center. You're invited to stroll through the Peace Plaza—it's home to the "I Have a Dream" World Peace Rose Garden, a reflecting pool, and the Behold Monument, a sculpture designed by Patrick Morelli of the ancient African ritual of lifting up a newborn child. Tours of the entire site are free and self-guided. (Tours of Dr. King's birth home do require free tickets and are led by park rangers.)

www.nps.gov/malu
Neighborhood: Sweet Auburn

TIP

Before your visit, download the podcast "In Their Words: Andrew Young on Auburn Avenue" for a guided tour through the Auburn Avenue Historical District. Ambassador Young provides history, tips, and personal experiences so you can get to know the sites along this famous street.

DIG DEEPER
AT THE NATIONAL CENTER FOR CIVIL AND HUMAN RIGHTS

To dig even deeper into the history of the civil rights movement in the American South—and human rights around the world—visit the National Center for Civil and Human Rights. Here you'll experience the progression of human civil rights across the globe displayed through powerful images, historical objects, and commanding audio showcased in a series galleries. See how Dr. Martin Luther King Jr. inspired social change when you view his own personal papers—they're part of a rotating exhibition from The Morehouse College Martin Luther King Jr. Collection in the Voice to the Voiceless gallery. The Spark of Conviction gallery features interactive technology to help you more appreciate human rights around the world, and realize how they affect every person. And to fully comprehend the struggles of the Civil Rights Movement of the 1950s and 1960s, the Rolls Down Like Water gallery includes visceral sights, sounds, and interactive exhibits depicting the March on Washington, Jim Crow laws, the Freedom Riders, the aftermath of the MLK assassination and more from those who fought for equal rights.

55 Ivan Allen Junior Boulevard, 404-991-6970,
www.civilandhumanrights.org
Neighborhood: Downtown

INSPIRE SOCIAL CHANGE
AT THE KING CENTER

While technically also part of the Martin Luther King Jr. National Historic Site, the King Center was established by Coretta Scott King in 1968 in memory of her husband and to serve "as a center of human endeavor, committed to the causes for which he lived and died." Millions visit the site every year to pay their respects to Dr. King and his late wife but also to study and research his papers and those of the Southern Christian Leadership Conference, the organization he founded. The King Library and Archives holds more records on Martin Luther King Jr. and the American civil rights movement than anywhere else in the world. Other objects belonging to Dr. and Mrs. King are also on display to the public as well as memorial exhibits devoted to Rosa Parks and Mahatma Gandhi.

449 Auburn Avenue, 404-526-8900, www.thekingcenter.org
Neighborhood: Sweet Auburn

BE BLOWN AWAY
BY THE ATLANTA BALLET

It's the country's oldest continually operating dance company, but that doesn't mean the Atlanta Ballet is old school. Sure, you can always see classical performances of *The Nutcracker*, *Swan Lake*, and *Romeo and Juliet*, but these dancers are constantly pushing boundaries with modern and contemporary performances as well. This is, after all, the ballet company that collaborated with Antwan "Big Boi" Patton of the Grammy Award–winning group OutKast. The cutting-edge show several years ago featured Atlanta Ballet dancers and hip-hop artists Big Boi, Sleepy Brown, Janelle Monáe, and more performing together—live. Old school? I don't think so.

1695 Marietta Boulevard, 404-892-3303,
www.atlantaballet.com
Neighborhood: The Westside

SEE AN AUTHENTIC PERFORMANCE
OF SHAKESPEARE

Even the Bard himself would approve of the live performances at the New American Shakespeare Tavern. The Atlanta Shakespeare Company prides itself on a theatrical approach called original practice, which means the plays you see here are performed as Shakespeare intended. Shows incorporate Elizabethan-style costumes, live sound effects, and period music all created by the company. Actors talk directly to the audience the way Shakespeare and his acting company would likely have addressed Elizabethan audience members. If you're a fan of Shakespeare, you can't get a more authentic experience than the one here.

499 Peachtree Street, 404-874-5299,
www.gashakespeare.org
Neighborhood: Midtown

FEEL FABULOUS
INSIDE THE FOX THEATRE

Sometimes Atlantans can do amazing things. And saving the landmark Fox Theatre from demolition in the '70s has to be one of those great achievements. Today, this majestic theater hosts some of the city's best Broadway shows, concerts, and live acts, and stands as a testament to an era when glamorous movie palaces were staples of the community. Taking in a performance here transports you to another world—the building's 1920s design was inspired by ancient temples of the Far East and is dominated by Egyptian- and Moorish-style domes and archways, gold leaf details, exquisite textiles, and trompe l'oeil art. Guided tours take you behind the scenes—everywhere from the orchestra pit to Mighty Mo, the largest working Moller theater organ in the world—and talk fun facts like how the theater's signature night sky ceiling with twinkling stars and wafting clouds is created.

660 Peachtree Street, 404-881-2100,
www.foxtheatre.org
Neighborhood: Midtown

DIG INTO DESIGN
AT MODA

Architecture, Italian motorcycles, and even skateboard graphics are among the range of exhibition topics at the Museum of Design Atlanta. You'd be hard pressed to find that kind of art anywhere else in town. And that's what makes MODA, well, MODA. It's the only museum in the entire Southeast devoted to the study and celebration of design. So if you see art in a paper clip or admire the iPod as a design solution, pencil in a trip to MODA, stat.

1315 Peachtree Street, 404-979-6455,
www.museumofdesign.org
Neighborhood: Midtown

STILL YOUR MIND
AT BAPS MANDIR

Mandir actually means "still" and "mind," and you'll definitely be rendered speechless by the stunning beauty of the 30,000-square-foot mandir in Lilburn. The traditional Hindu place of worship is made of more than 106,000 cubic feet of white Italian marble, Turkish limestone, and Indian pink sandstone, plus 34,000 handmade carvings shipped from India. This veritable work of art is open to the public for social, cultural, and spiritual activities—an audio tour explains in fascinating detail the stories behind its Hindu art, architecture, and philosophy.

460 Rockbridge Road, Lilburn, 678-906-2277,
www.baps.org/atlanta
Neighborhood: Lilburn

TOUR THE OVAL OFFICE
AT THE JIMMY CARTER
LIBRARY AND MUSEUM

It's probably about as close as you'll ever get to stepping foot in the actual one—and this Oval Office is totally realistic. The full-scale model looks exactly like it did when Jimmy Carter was president, right down to the paint color on the walls. New exhibitions throughout the museum (it underwent a massive overhaul in 2009) allow you to track President Carter's life from Plains, Georgia, to Pennsylvania Avenue.

441 Freedom Parkway, 404-865-7100,
www.jimmycarterlibrary.gov
Neighborhood: Poncey-Highland

MAKE THE NEWS
AT CNN

We're not suggesting that you cause trouble and end up the top story on CNN. Just take one of the Atlanta-based news network's behind-the-scenes tours. And there are several, including one centered on HLN's popular show Morning Express with Robin Meade. You visit the newsroom and control room, watch a portion of the live broadcast, and meet with anchor Robin Meade.

One CNN Center, 404-827-2300,
www.cnn.com/tour
Neighborhood: Downtown

WALK LIKE AN EGYPTIAN
AT THE MICHAEL C. CARLOS MUSEUM

Get more than a glimpse into ancient Egypt with the collection of antiquities at the Michael C. Carlos Museum. This treasured museum at Emory University houses exhibitions that cover the entire Nile Valley civilization, including original artifacts obtained in Egypt by Emory professor William Shelton in 1920 and the oldest Egyptian mummy in the country. The museum also houses extraordinary collections and artifacts from ancient Greece, Rome, the Near East, Asia, and sub-Saharan Africa.

571 South Kilgo Circle, 404-727-4282,
www.carlos.emory.edu
Neighborhood: Druid Hills/Emory Village

LISTEN
TO PUBLIC ART

You can easily go to Andrew Young Plaza downtown and view the bronze Andrew Young Obelisk created by artist Curtis Patterson. But dial into the Office of Cultural Affairs' Public Art Audio Tour at 404-260-5532 (or download the Atlanta Public Art Tour app from the app store) and you'll hear both Andrew Young and Curtis Patterson speaking. Andrew Young Plaza is stop No. 1 of twenty-two of the city's public art collection that you can view while listening to interesting interviews and historical information via your phone or app. Simply download the map beforehand from the Atlanta Office of Cultural Affairs' website, and you'll be in the know about some of the city's most historically significant pieces of public art.

www.ocaatlanta.com

GIVE A DAMN
AT THE MARGARET MITCHELL HOUSE AND MUSEUM

Apartment No. 1 is a far cry from Tara, but it's where author Margaret Mitchell brought Rhett, Ashley, and Scarlett to life when she wrote her Pulitzer Prize–winning novel, *Gone With the Wind*. The tiny apartment she called "the dump" is located in a Tudor-revival building on Peachtree Street now listed on the National Register of Historic Places. The interior has been restored and includes exhibits about Mitchell and her famous novel. Her apartment was returned to its former 1930s state, preserving its original architectural features and leaded glass windows.

990 Peachtree Street, 404-249-7015,
www.margaretmitchellhouse.com
Neighborhood: Midtown

SHOOT FOR THE STARS
AT THE FERNBANK SCIENCE CENTER
OBSERVATORY

The Big Dipper will forever seem like small change compared to what you'll see from the thirty-foot dome of the Fernbank Science Center's Dr. Ralph L. Buice, Jr. Observatory. It is the largest in the Southeast and is open to the public—for free!—Thursday and Friday nights when the weather cooperates. Hit a celestial show at the planetarium beforehand and you're in for a twinkling treat.

156 Heaton Park Drive, 678-874-7102,
www.fernbank.edu
Neighborhood: Druid Hills

SLIP AWAY
TO SERENBE

Spend a day or a weekend at this charming, eco-minded community south of Atlanta to rejuvenate, be one with nature, or just enjoy your family. Rent a bike and make your way through Selborne Lane's quaint shops and galleries, then stop for a cup of coffee and a pastry at the Blue Eyed Daisy Bakeshop. Equestrians can saddle up and experience Serenbe's rolling hills and countryside on horseback, then end the day at the spa recuperating from the ride. Popular activities are ongoing year-round, including May Day, Southern Chefs Potluck, Afternoon in the Country, and live performances at the Serenbe Playhouse. Several award-winning restaurants, including The Hil and the Farmhouse at Serenbe, are worth the visit alone.

www.serenbe.com
Neighborhood: Chattahoochee Hills

GO STRAIGHT TO JAIL
WITH HOSEA FEED THE HUNGRY

Of course we're not suggesting you get locked up. That would just be silly. But you know you're always looking for ways to avoid your kitchen (and family perhaps?) on Thanksgiving Eve, so the obvious solution is to join families you don't know in the kitchen of the DeKalb County Jail to help prep a Thanksgiving meal for Atlanta's hungry and homeless. You won't deal with any whining or complaining from anyone here; you don't even really need cooking skills—just a good attitude and a willingness to help. And the diners who'll be feasting on your Thanksgiving spread will be among the most grateful you have ever served.

www.4hosea.org
Neighborhood: Decatur

TIP
Can't commit during Thanksgiving? No worries.
Hosea Feed the Hungry needs volunteers beyond the holiday season,
so you can donate your time throughout the year.

ENTER THE ATLANTA OPEN
ORTHOGRAPHIC MEET

This annual competition pits some of Atlanta's brightest against, well, anyone else who has the guts to sign up for what is your basic childhood nightmare: a spelling bee. It has been ongoing since 1971 (that's right) and includes four rounds of doing your best to spell words like bokeh and vellicate. Think you're smart enough to compete with the big dogs? The bee is held the Saturday after Valentine's Day at Poncey-Highland hangout Manuel's Tavern and is free to those who actually think they have a chance.

602 North Highland Avenue,
www.atlantaopenorthographicmeet.com
Neighborhood: Poncey-Highland

ENCOUNTER ATLANTA'S PAST
AT OAKLAND CEMETERY

You can learn a lot about Atlanta by strolling through historic Oakland Cemetery. It's the resting place of some of the city's most famous residents—Pulitzer Prize–winning author Margaret Mitchell; golf legend Bobby Jones; Bishop Wesley John Gaines, founder of Morris Brown College; six Georgia governors; and twenty-seven Atlanta mayors—as well as many more not-so-famous. Maps at the Visitors Center or two free iPhone apps provide rich historical details and paths to follow for a self-guided stroll. But it's more fun to go with a guide. Many tours are offered (even Twilight Tours) and tell the stories behind Oakland's most famous residents, architectural monuments, and fascinating epitaphs.

248 Oakland Avenue, 404-688-2107,
www.oaklandcemetery.com
Neighborhood: Cabbagetown

TIP

Other famous Georgians, including Asa G. Candler, founder of Coca-Cola; Joel Chandler Harris, author of the Uncle Remus stories; Atlanta mayors William Hartsfield and I. N. Ragsdale; Frank L. Stanton, poet laureate of Georgia; and Robert Woodruff, philanthropist and former president of Coca-Cola, are all buried at historic Westview Cemetery.

1680 Westview Drive, 404-755-6611, www.westviewcemetery.com

DRIVE BACK IN TIME
AT OLD CAR CITY USA

You know what they say: One man's trash is another man's treasure. Well, what started as a junkyard in 1931 may very well be one of the coolest places we know to photograph classic cars. Granted, most are dilapidated, rusted, and covered in pine straw, but that's part of the charm of Old Car City. Walking this massive junkyard is like taking a trip back in time to the golden age of the American automobile—and it's a photographer's dream. Here you can snap supercool shots of classic Ford, Cadillac, Chevy, Buick, and Oldsmobile cars from every era—we're talking Fairlanes, T-Birds, Skylarks, Bel Airs. The owners claim that if the car was built before 1975, they likely have at least a few somewhere on the thirty-four acres.

3098 Highway 411, White, 770-382-6141,
www.oldcarcityusa.com

GOD BLESS THE ANIMALS
AT THE CATHEDRAL OF ST. PHILIP

So your dog training sessions aren't going so well, and you're certain you have a hound from hell? (Trust me, I understand.) You may want to enlist the help of a higher power. Thank heavens the Cathedral of St. Philip welcomes your four-legged family members to attend services on the first Sunday of every October. To honor the Feast of St. Francis, your dog (and other furry friends) receives blessings from the church canons right there inside the cathedral. Now as much as we want to believe these blessings can perform miracles, in this case you probably don't want to cancel your dog's obedience classes—just yet anyway.

2744 Peachtree Road, 404-365-1000,
www.stphilipscathedral.org
Neighborhood: Buckhead

SHOPPING AND FASHION

DRESS TO IMPRESS
AT JEFFREY FASHION CARES

It's not every day you get the chance to see a swanky runway show in Atlanta. It's even rarer when it's one that brings together high fashion and philanthropy. What is profound, though, is the kind of cash that style aficionado Jeffrey Kalinsky, owner of Jeffrey boutiques in Atlanta and New York City, has managed to raise since 1992—about $11 million for the Atlanta AIDS Fund and Susan G. Komen for the Cure's Greater Atlanta affiliate. You, fashionista, get to have all the fun. Come dressed to impress, see the season's hottest looks from designers like Lanvin, Prada, Balenciaga, and Christian Louboutin walk the runway, and then bid in the live auction (how does a trip to New York Fashion Week and a tour of the *Vogue* offices sound?). Do it! It's for charity.

www.jeffreyfashioncares.com

SHOP STAR PROVISIONS

This food lover's mecca is a culinarian's dream come true. The charming gourmet market on the Westside is owned by famed chef Anne Quatrano, and she has stocked it with the best of the best. Want dry-aged beef? She's got it. Fresh farm eggs? You will find them here. Homemade charcuterie? It is fresh-made and sold here, too. Cheesemonger Carolyn Bender keeps more than two hundred varieties of cheese in stock and features more Southern cheeses than anybody else in the country. Star Provisions also sells super-cute tableware, great cookbooks, wine, gourmet coffee, olive oil, vinegar, and more. The bakery sells hot and cold prepared foods and a slew of retro candy.

1198 Howell Mill Road, 404-365-0410,
www.starprovisions.com
Neighborhood: The Westside

SHOP TILL YOU DROP

If there's one thing you can do in Atlanta, it's drop some serious cash at the cash register. And the first place fashionistas flock to spend their dough is Buckhead—it's home to the most prominent malls in the South—Lenox Square and Phipps Plaza. Here shoppers have their pick of some of the country's best retail and department stores—think Neiman Marcus, Saks Fifth Avenue, Tory Burch, Gucci, Burberry, Cartier, and Louis Vuitton, while upscale boutiques like Lululemon, Bill Hallman, and Tootsies are just across the street at the Shops Around Lenox.

Across town the best shopping is in the Westside Provisions District. Delicious home decor stores like Bungalow Classic, Jonathan Adler, Knoll, Kolo Collection, and Room & Board mix with specialty fashion stores such as Billy Reid, Sid and Ann Mashburn, Free People, and G. Gilbert. If you want to look good, these guys can make it happen.

Yes, we love our big malls and chic retailers in Atlanta, but we also adore our local artists. The city is full of cool co-ops and funky markets where these creative types sell their goods, and we buy them in droves. The Beehive in Edgewood, HomeGrown in Decatur, and the quarterly Root City Market pop-up in the Old Fourth Ward sell some of the coolest wares you'll find, well, anywhere.

● ●

TIP

If you're looking for ultra high-end shopping (à la Rodeo Drive) hit the eight-acre Shops Buckhead Atlanta. The walkable, über-posh retail shopping collection located at Peachtree and East Paces Ferry roads includes best-in-class brands—think Hermès, Christian Louboutin, and Dior— and designer boutiques like Billy Reid.

www.theshopsbuckheadatlanta.com

Lenox Square
3393 Peachtree Road, 404-233-6767,
www.simon.com/mall/lenox-square

Phipps Plaza
3500 Peachtree Road, 404-261-7910,
www.simon.com/mall/phipps-plaza

Shops Around Lenox
3400 Around Lenox Drive,
www.shopsaroundlenox.com

Westside Provisions District
1100 Howell Mill Road, 404-872-7538,
www.westsidepd.com

HomeGrown Decatur
412 Church Street, Decatur, 404-373-1147,
www.homegrowndecatur.com

The Beehive
1250 Caroline Street, Suite C120, 404-581-9261,
www.thebeehiveatl.com

Root City Market
112 Krog Street, www.rootcitymarket.com

DIG DEEP
AT WAX 'N' FACTS

Crate after crate of new and vintage vinyl have filled this store in the heart of Little Five Points since 1976. You won't have to dig long to find your favorites—the selection runs deep and includes rock, soul, funk, hip-hop. You name it. They probably have it (or can get it).

432 Moreland Avenue, 404-525-2275,
www.waxnfacts.com
Neighborhood: Little Five Points

TIP
Criminal Records Atlanta is another stellar independent vinyl store in town. It is just around the cornerin Little Five Points, so if you're on a music mission, don't pass it by.
1154-A Euclid Avenue, 404-215-9511,
www.criminalatl.com

PICK YOUR VEGGIES
AT THE PEACHTREE ROAD FARMERS MARKET

Is there anything James Beard Award–winning chef Linton Hopkins cannot do? He owns Restaurant Eugene, Holeman & Finch Public House, Linton's in the Garden, H&F Burger, and Hop's Chicken. But he also cofounded the wildly popular Peachtree Road Farmers Market with his wife, Gina, and Dean Sam Candler and Vicar George Maxwell of the Cathedral of St. Philip in 2007. The market features products grown, raised, or made by the sellers—think farm eggs, breads and pastries, artisan cheeses, fresh milk, fair-trade coffee, and even art. Live demos from the city's best chefs and special programs for the kids add fun social elements.

The Cathedral of St. Philip, 2744 Peachtree Road,
www.peachtreeroadfarmersmarket.com
Neighborhood: Buckhead

Atlanta is a big city, and nearly every neighborhood has its own market, which means you can buy from vendors close to home or venture out and see what's growing outside your neck of the woods.

Alpharetta Farmers Market
Saturdays, April to mid-October, Old Canton Street, Alpharetta, www.alpharettafarmersmarket.com

Decatur Farmers Market
Wednesdays, March to October, 163 Clairemont Avenue, Decatur; Saturdays, year-round, 498 North McDonough Street, Decatur, www.decaturfarmersmarket.com

East Atlanta Village Farmers Market
Thursdays, mid-April to mid-December, 561 Flat Shoals Avenue, www.farmeav.com

Green Market at Piedmont Park
Saturdays, March to mid-December, Piedmont Park's
12th Street entrance gate,
www.piedmontpark.org

Marietta Square Farmers Market
Saturdays, year-round; Sundays, April to November,
65 Church Street, Marietta Square,
www.mariettasquarefarmersmarket.net

Morningside Farmers' Market
Saturdays, year-round, 1393 North Highland Avenue,
www.morningsidemarket.com

Serenbe Farmers Artist Market
Saturdays, May to October, 8457 Atlanta Newnan
Road, Chattahoochee Hills,
www.serenbefarms.com

HUNT FOR TREASURE
AT SCOTT ANTIQUE MARKET

Savvy shoppers know that on the second weekend of every month you head south of the city to Scott Antique Market. It's the largest indoor antiques show in the country and is spread across two massive buildings (the South building sells less expensive items than the North). Dealers are typically located in the same spots from month to month, making them easy to locate again and again. You never know what you might find here, either; treasures include everything from vintage prints and sterling silver to custom wood furniture and retro upholstered pieces.

3650 Jonesboro Road (North building),
3850 Jonesboro Road (South building),
www.scottantiquemarket.com

SHOP SWEET AUBURN
CURB MARKET

Atlanta has shopped for fresh produce here since sellers first set up on the curb in 1918. In the 1920s, it moved to its current location, but because of segregation, blacks were still allowed to only shop from the stalls on the curb (hence the name). Today, everyone's welcome, and you can find just about anything here, from local and organic vegetables from a variety of vendors, specialty and gourmet foods and fresh pastries, desserts, and breads. Restaurants like Bell Street Burritos, Grindhouse Killer Burgers, and Sweet Auburn Barbecue all have cult followings.

209 Edgewood Avenue,
www.sweetauburncurbmarket.com
Neighborhood: Sweet Auburn District

• •

SUGGESTED
ITINERARIES

MUSTS FOR MUSIC LOVERS

Atlanta Jazz Festival, 52

Eddie's Attic, 42

Metalsome Karaoke at the 10 High, 40

Music Midtown, 55

Northside Tavern, 37

Wax 'n' Facts, 124

WINE AND DINE

Atlanta Food & Wine Festival, 8

Atlanta Food Truck Park, 6

BaconFest, 23

Brick Store Pub, 20

Feast on Fried Chicken, 26

Ice Cream, 16

Krispy Kreme, 12

Krog Street Market, 9

Nuevo Laredo Cantina, 22

Pig Out on Barbecue, 28

Praise Southern Food, 24

Shop Star Provisions, 119

The Sun Dial, 14

Sweet Auburn Curb Market, 129

SweetWater Brewery, 10

The Varsity, 2

• •

CULTURAL CLASSICS

ONLY IN ATLANTA

SPORTS SPOTS

THE GREAT OUTDOORS

HISTORICAL OUTPOSTS

KID FRIENDLY

ACTIVITIES
BY SEASON

You'll always find tons of fun in Atlanta every weekend of the year. But some of the city's best events happen only once annually, while others are just better during specific seasons. We've pulled together some of our favorites according to when they're best to attend.

SPRING

Atlanta Food & Wine Festival, 8

Atlanta Moon Ride, 65

Atlanta Botanical Garden, 50

BaconFest, 23

Dogwood Festival, 46

Piedmont Park Dog Park, 78

Silver Comet Trail, 69

Starlight Drive-in Theatre, 36

SUMMER

Atlanta Jazz Festival, 52

Bike the BeltLine, 70

Fountain of Rings at Centennial Olympic Park, 72

Get in a Braves Game, 62

Jeffrey Fashion Cares, 118

Run the Peachtree Road Race, 66

Scream for Ice Cream, 16

Tour SweetWater Brewery, 10

Shoot the Hooch, 67

FALL

WINTER

INDEX